An Unlikely Predator

by S.C. Gray

Published by Sojourner Publishing

Published by Sojourner Publishing

Dedicated to
people of any age group who find
themselves in the situation
described in this book
and
to people who suspect a friend or
family member might have fallen
prey to an unlikely predator

An Unlikely Predator

Table of Contents

FORWARD

I hear young people announce their future with confidence:

After high school graduation, I'm attending the University of Georgia to major in business administration. If possible, I'll continue my studies to obtain a Master's Degree. Then, I will begin my career with a job paying at least $70,000.00 with benefits, of course. Bold plans on the horizon bring hope and enthusiasm for announced future intentions. Every parent's bright star moment arises. Every parent feels pride as the proof of maturity appears in career choice and college plans are verbalized by their child. The steps toward independence begins.

At any time during the climb toward his worthy goal, snags can occur to change a well-constructed plan. Interest may wane in the major subject matter. An undisciplined roommate plays havoc with study time. A certain professor lacks teaching skills but gives killer tests. From my experience, these examples demonstrate typical snags in the life of a college or new career person.

What if communication with the family stops? When a conversation does occur, what if a change in habit is detected? What if a certain person's name, an unfamiliar name, is repeated often during a phone conversation? Is this person a new boyfriend or girlfriend? No, he or she is just a friend.

Certainly, it's unfair to assume the worst with every
scenario I described.
However, if these questions ring true, it's fair to assume
something different is happening.
Some of us find ourselves as easy prey for
an unlikely predator.

An Unlikely Predator
by S.C. Gray

Chapter 1

Surprise and Shock

She pulled back the sheet and slipped in beside me. "I was afraid I'd bump Donald's knee," she explained as her body found mine. With movements akin to familiarity, she pressed her body against my back, her arm encircling me. Rolling me over, she kissed me with fervor and urgency. As her hands explored my body, my senses awakened and heated to an extent I'd never felt before. The surprise of it left me in total shock. Was this really happening? My aunt's best friend? This woman two years older than my mother? Is this what my aunt and Hilda did togeth-er? So many questions flashed through my mind as the kisses grew more passionate. I thought about her husband, but then he'd just had surgery. She didn't act worried about anyone seeing her with me. I thought about her children coming into the living room, but evidently caution didn't enter her mind. Even with these worries floating through my mind, I "came" in a very short time.

Believe it or not, I had never experience such aggression. Yes, I dated boys in high school and men while attending college. One guy at the university became rather pushy but pulled back after my negative response. This woman didn't ask, didn't hint about anything sexual during the evening, and didn't know me personally. She treated me with special status because my aunt was her best friend. By special status, I'm referring to the dinner invitation. Other than polite dinner and evening conversation, I had never spoken at length with her. What triggered her actions toward me? I didn't consider myself gay. By primari-ly following my dad around because Mother suffered the consequences of polio, I learned what might be considered "man's work" and folks perceived me as a tom boy. Enjoying outdoor activities and knowing how to use a wrench didn't label me in the lesbian category. I'd had boyfriends since the second grade.

I had seen Hilda two different times in West Texas with my aunt and family. Because of her outgoing personality and my aunt's matching personality, the two talked with animation and plenty of laugher. They caught my attention with their jovial conversations that dominated any other conversing taking place in the room.

If a husband traveled with her or children were present, my memory goes almost blank. However, I know they were present.

I hadn't planned to spend the night, but after being invited, and thinking about the lonely bedroom in a strange house in a strange neighborhood, I accepted the invitation.

Later I learned the two potted chrysan-themums I'd taken her as a thank you for the dinner invitation, were interpreted by her as a forward gesture with sexual overtones. Two six inch potted chrysanthemums with discard-ed newspaper wrapping brought from the Six Flags Over Georgia greenhouse, had meant much more than a "bread and butter" gift to this gray-headed, middle-aged woman.

Chapter 2

Arrival in Area

Backing up in time three or four days, my cousin and I entered the city limits of Austell, Georgia the day after my graduation from the University of Georgia. Don't ask me how this happened, but we reached the Grey Hound Bus Station in Atlanta without incident. Not an easy task for two country kids. We parked my white 1962 Dodge Dart beside the Grey Hound Bus Station where Dave ended his thirty day leave from the Army. My cousin returned to active duty, and I prepared for my first job as a college graduate.

Following written directions, I soon parked my car near the entry of what looked like a residential dwelling in Austell. Confidence returned when I spotted the business name clearly displayed on a wooden sign. My surprise at seeing the humble home of Burkshire Real Estate dissipated with the enthusiastic greeting of my aunt's best friend Hilda. After her warm reception, she led me to her husband's office explaining he would help me find a place to live. I didn't sense any enthusiasm in his demeanor toward me. But, then he just didn't seem like a very enthusiastic person. Because I wished to keep down expenses, I suggested finding a room to rent. In no time at all, he found an ad in the Austell paper for a room to rent. He placed a call, arranged an appointment for me, and wrote down her address. As I stood to leave his office, he said something nebulous about maybe seeing me sometime. I drove away a bit disappointed since I didn't know a soul in Austell, Georgia, and he didn't show interest in future contact.

The street lined with small frame houses, neat appearing with simple landscaping and neatly mowed yards, greeted me as I turned on Fourteenth Street. Mrs. Cox invited me into her nondescript living room where everything looked beige.

After a pleasant conversation, she quoted a monthly price for the bedroom including a private bathroom down the hall. She had already cleared some shelf space in the kitchen cabinets and refrigerator. Although, I wasn't looking forward to cooking very much. I unloaded most of my worldly possessions consisting of a couple of suitcases and a couple of cardboard boxes. Thus embarking on my first place of residence as a working adult. The "on my own" phase of life had begun.

Chapter 3

First Day at Work

Somewhat excited and somewhat scared, I found my place of employment the next morn-ing. I'd spent a day at Six Flags Over Georgia with a group of high school friends a few years back, but entering the back gate as an employee suited me. The greenhouse impressed me with its size and abundance of colorful bedding plants and humongous hanging baskets. Someone directed me to Chip Summer's office, the landscape architect for Six Flags. I must have looked as green as the plants, but I arrived with the job secured because of a recommendation from Dr. Suther, head of the horticulture department at the university. As an alumni, Chip welcomed me graciously and showed me the ropes, so to speak. Part of my orientation that first day included meeting the two men under my supervision and accompanying Chip on a tour of this grand greenhouse, now under my supervision. My two helpers, at least twice my age or more, appeared friendly enough, but I detected some uncertainty in their eyes. Their new supervisor, not only "green behind the ears," but a female. Beyond a doubt, I knew their thoughts.

The word work entered my brain. "Yes, work," I thought. That first day I made huge, colorful baskets of petunias, coleus, periwinkles, and wandering jew. Perlite beds with a mist system stood ready for cuttings. Plant cuttings were a big deal in the horticulture business because of the money saved. Starting a plant from a cutting instead of buying a potted plant didn't compare in cost especially when utilizing a vast quantity of plant material. I made cuttings of coleus and begonias demonstrating my knowledge by working. As I worked along side these men, they began warming up to me by talking. Talking comes cheap, they say; yet on this particular day, talking meant acceptance. From that day on we shared a compatible working situation. The importance and the huge scale of the plant operation began sinking into my head that first day as well. Hilda called me shortly after arriving back at Mrs. Cox's house. After that monumental first day at Six Flags, an invitation to dinner the next evening sounded perfect. Great! I had a home cooked meal coming my way - still thinking with a college student mentality.

After my second full day at the green-house, I looked forward to visiting the Burkshires. Remembering my home training, I racked my brain for the thought of some gift to take my hostess. What better gift than flowers? They surrounded me. Finding a couple of chrysan-themums not scheduled for baskets, I wrapped the pots properly with newspaper since floral wrap didn't exist in the greenhouse. At least I had something to take as a "bread and butter gift." Surely I paid for those chrysanthemums!

Chapter 4

The First Visit

Following the directions to the northeast side of Austell , I pulled my college car into a dirt and gravel area near the house. The appear-ance of the house surprised me. We lived in a white stucco house at the farm, but it looked fresh and in good repair. This house needed repair. Even miles from any town, my dad had constructed a gravel driveway, a fenced in front yard, and a sidewalk to both the front and back doors. This lady, I thought, ran a successful real estate business, and I assumed her husband helped bring in business at the real estate office. So, my first impression of the frame house in need of some repair seemed contradictory somehow. I rationalized my presumptuous thinking away, however.

A lively welcome further pushed the house thing from my mind. I stood at the screen door with the two yellow potted chrysanthemums. Hilda took them from me with exclamations of thanks and a big hug.

Whatever reserve I had felt from her husband dissipated with the warmth of her welcome. Her happy, friendly children followed her exam-ple, so I felt completely at ease. I did remember meeting her children at least once before when the Burkshire family visited my aunt and uncle in Southern Georgia. They weren't exactly children any-more at twelve and thirteen. Keith, followed by his sister one year later, was the older of the two. I enjoyed the kids. We developed an immediate rapport as I watched some of Keith's antics with various facial expressions. An enjoyable evening for me consisted for the most part of a home cooked meal. During my four years of college life, home cooked food had earned a new respect. And, just a few days into my "adult" life, I hadn't even shopped at a grocery store. So far, my cup-board in Mrs. Cox's kitchen remained empty.

I don't remember dinner. We ate, of course, but nothing stands out in my memory about that meal. I do remember Donald's absence, but she explained that he had just undergone knee surgery. After lively conversations with Keith and Ruth, they eventually said goodnight. I'd seen their bedrooms soon after I arrived and was not impressed with either one. Keith's bedroom lay between the kitchen and master bedroom look-ing more like a wide hallway rather than a bed-room. Ruth's small and uninteresting bedroom caught my eye because my bedroom at home, which I shared with one of my sisters, had rock maple furniture, a green floral bed spread, short beige curtains Mother had sewn, and various decorations we had acquired. My plastic red clock radio from Christmas 1961, and a prized 8X10 picture of my boyfriend finished our room with a flare. The memory of my bedroom caused me to notice the lack of decorations.

The next day meant work. Combined with the tiredness I felt both physically and emotionally from my first day of work, I greeted the announcement of the living room divan as my bed for the night. Hilda lifted a handle un-derneath the couch that made the couch into a bed. Except for a valley running down the middle of the sofa bed, it was doable. As a kid I had encountered "the crack" at various kinfolk overnight stays and knew I'd be all right as long as I avoided the crack down the middle. We spread a blanket ever the divan first, then a bottom and top sheet. Hilda left, I pulled on borrowed pajamas, and switched off a nearby lamp. Well, then came the surprise I described earlier. All these years later, I feel startled when I think about that moment, the moment when she slid between the sheets. Could I have foreseen the major disaster thundering toward me like a a herd of wild horses, I would have run to my little college car and sped away.

Chapter 5

Back to Work

An alarm of some sort must have been set, because we got up in time for some cereal and my morning clock-in at Six Flags. Needing focus for my new job, I set the incredible thoughts of the night aside. Taking 24" wire baskets, sphagnum moss, a light weight soil mixture, and blooming bedding plants, we created colorful hanging baskets that decorated the entire park. I learned to drive a cart through the park picking up hanging baskets beyond their peak and replacing them with fresh, perky baskets. This fun task initiated my first days as I began learning other responsibilities accompanying the job.

The necessity of moving pallets of bedding plants called for a broad walkway in the greenhouse wide enough for a small Bobcat. That white Bobcat fascinated me, and I did learn to drive it. Pallets of flowers were delivered to decorate the park with color. Wooden flats of petunias, marigolds, begonias, coleus, and other colorful bedding plants arrived at least twice a week. Every flat of plants had a mission either to create impressive hanging baskets or to cover large outdoor areas with color.

In the middle of the day as I looked over a new shipment of flowers, I turned around to find Hilda watching me with eyes full of total adoration. I glanced around for the men. Had they seen her and caught her look? I showed her around, introduced her to my two charges, and walked her to the large greenhouse entry. She insisted I come for dinner again. Did she mention anything about spending the night? I'm sure she did. As a red-blooded American girl, the passion drew me in and fascinated me. This woman, my aunt's best friend, pulled me in with her outgoing personality and smooth charisma.

My landlady seldom saw me. I came to pick up clothes, and once in a while I spent the night. My dad contacted me somehow by phone one evening when I happened to spend the night at Mrs. Cox's house. He had called for me a day or so before, and Mrs. Cox just happened to mention the fact that she rarely saw me. Why was that the case, he wanted to know? I mentioned how warm and friendly the Burkshires treated me and how they welcomed me into their home. He knew they carried on a strong friendship with my aunt and uncle, so I played on that. I could tell he thought staying in my own rented place a better plan. Even though I had graduated from college and had begun succeeding in my employment opportunity, I owed much to my folks. The majority of my monetary support through college came from them.

Out of respect for them, I made a concerted effort to spend more nights in my first abode. My kitchen shelves took on a new look. I bought cans of soup, beanie weenies, tuna, bread, and pop tarts. My refrigerator space, I partially filled with milk, orange juice, and Dr. Peppers. Did I buy eggs or bacon or butter? I doubt it. Anytime I stayed in my room, I bored myself. Watching TV with Mrs. Cox bored me further. I felt lonely in that house.

Chapter 6

Church

From about the second weekend, I began attending church with Hilda and her family. I met them at a small brick church on the west side of Atlanta. The same denomination as my aunt and uncle, I had some knowledge and experience with this group. Members accepted me immediately since I was Ruth's niece, the beloved vocalist with a vivacious personality. Hilda's clout in the church appeared obvious. She lead some hymns as the congregation sang in harmonious acappella style. Other members lead songs, also. Singing certainly a major part of the service finally lead to sermon time, which lasted well after 12 noon. After the service, I met other friendly, warm people who were thrilled by my attendance. Some of those people became great friends throughout the years. The men definitely played the dominate role in this church. No thought whatsoever was given to the ordination of an elder or a deacon as a woman's role. Such roles were served by men only. The reason I stress this point lies in the particular part Hilda played in this male dominated leadership. Often when a group of men stood discussing church matters, one woman usually appeared in the group. Hilda. Her confidence in identifying with male leadership and projecting herself as an integral personality in the group separated her as unique among the women. Sometimes I wondered how the men felt about her involvement.

Much to the chagrin of my parents, I soon joined that church making a huge departure from my upbringing. My family was part of that group described as in church "every time the doors were opened." Striking differences between these denominations didn't detour me. For instance, the difference between singing with musical instrument accompaniment or singing acappella didn't lead the list of differences but was the most obvious. The folks at Fellowship just knew my joining was God's intent. After all, my aunt and uncle were devoted members of this group. Of course, the church brought another avenue of being with Hilda thus feeding my growing dependence on her.

Chapter 7

Work Involvement

Filling the large perlite automatic mist beds with cuttings keep us busy at the greenhouse. Although not a difficult procedure to create a cutting, one must have the knowledge to cut in just the right place on a stem. Coleus grew rapidly from cuttings and filled the large wire baskets with their sun loving array of colorful leaves. The thousands of bedding plants delivered to the greenhouse ranged from petunias to marigolds. We maintained these lovely visitors until the night crew took flats and flats and more flats, stripped out the beds full of faded flowers, and replanted with the fresh ones. Overnight dramatic changes occurred in flower bed displays all over the park. The Six Flags landscape architect Mr. Summers orchestrated the grand design.

I ventured through the summer in a surreal state of mind as I labored in an enjoyable job coupled with the surprises of Hilda's visits to take me to lunch or to give me an invitation to spend the night. In fact, we soon graduated to Ruth's bedroom. Where did Ruth sleep? I'm not sure, but I think in Keith's so-called bedroom. I didn't ask, because the bed brought much more comfort. Surely the excuse for not sleep-ing with Donald had worn out; she seemed not to worry about that. After all, what did he contribute to the family? Precious little I soon realized. Each night with Hilda fired the same passion as the very first night. Her appetite nev-er waned. I was hooked. One weekend after I'd spent the night with Hilda, some church friends from another town dropped in. I was still in bed. A young woman, probably near my age, came into the bedroom and said something to me about being careful because Hilda liked young-er women. Embarrassment crept over me, but I tried to disguise it and mumbled something to her.

My summer job, which had become more challenging as the summer progressed, gained momentum as my last month ensued. My new assignment consisted of visiting all six areas of the park, drawing a rough diagram of the plant-ings, making labels for each plant detailing the names, then transferring that information to a stake. Of course, since I created the markers and knew the plants, I then located each stake near the correct plant. This project must have taken the better part of a month. Some years later when I visited the park, I saw some of those stakes still in place.

Chapter 8

Hilda's Plan

The summer drew closer and closer to an end. Hilda announced a plan to me one afternoon. She had discovered a nursery in Austell for lease. Her mind and her plan was set. According to her, this was what I needed to do. We made an appointment to meet with the Briggs and discuss lease possibilities. Hilda did most of the talking. As a realtor she had experience with this sort of business.

A day or two later Mr. Summers offered me permanent employment with Six Flags, but I was already enamored with the idea of having my own business. After all, growing up on a family farm, the idea of having my own business seemed logical. Looking back, of course, the offer from Six Flags was such a compliment and the route I should have taken. But, Hilda had the wheels rolling. Nothing stopped this aggressive woman.

Before I knew what I was doing or thinking, my dad drove to Austell, met with the Briggs, met with a banker and cosigned a note with me, then left me to my own recognizance. Somehow Hilda never appeared while my dad helped set up the means for this business venture. When I look back at that situation, I cannot believe my dad cosigned that note enabling me to begin the operation of a business. My parents planned to give me a flight to Australia as a college graduation gift at my request. That dream of a visit to Australia switched to requesting help to launch a plant nursery business.

Why wasn't he fiercely opposed to the whole idea? He didn't, though. He made arrange-ments for a 50' mobile home delivered and placed at the nursery for my living quarters. Af-ter he left, Hilda took over again.

Chapter 9

The Nursery

A new sign on the property advertised Austell Nursery covering up the old name of Briggs Nursery. Now my thoughts were filled with plants and chemicals and components for potting mixture and gallon cans and saw dust and the list never ended. I sought the Briggs' advice for placing my first plant order. That created my second mistake. The first mistake was obvious. Controlled by Hilda's plans, I just filled in the blanks with my horticulture knowledge.

Back to the Briggs, they guided me from their experience of the past year. Ordering plant material as advised by the Briggs became my second mistake. Plants arrived from several sources, and guess who had to organize them correctly and water them every day as the sweltering summer heat threatened their existence?

Bare rooted plants required immediate planting in either a one gallon or five gallon can. I placed ground covers, shrubs, and trees in sun or shade categories. The plants had to stay alive and healthy for customer sales.

Work? Yes, almost beyond my capability. My horticulture knowledge held me in that re-gard, but I knew nothing about business per se. With no training in bookkeeping, I kept terrible records and didn't really have time to maintain proper books. My front yard consisted of the nursery, my residential phone and my business phone where one in the same. The business lived with me; I lived with the business. Why did people call at eight o'clock in the evening to ask a plant related question? Of course, later I learned not to answer the phone. I began collecting one gallon cans from two school cafeterias in Austell. Plastic containers did not exist at the time, so metal cans were bought and dipped in a tar solution to keep them from rust-ing. Hilda and I left the nursery at 4:30 in the morning one time each week to collect cans using her husband's pickup. Some very long days followed. Soon after I hired Amberto, I began soliciting builder's landscape jobs, which usually consisted of five or seven shrubs and two trees. Since we needed to stay at the nursery all day, the landscape jobs were installed after hours.

Six Flags Over Georgia hadn't forgotten about me. An offer to complete a project at Six Flags Over Texas surprised and encouraged me. Could I make a chart of all plant material in the park as I had processed for Six Flags Over Georgia? someone else would make the labels and affix them to the stakes if I could make the blue print. My job entailed supplying common, scientific, and family name for each plant. I agreed. Flying in a corporate jet with ultra comfortable seats was a treat I never expected. However, the physical surroundings could not compete with the company of another passenger. This charismatic man used the word <u>opportunity</u> countless times throughout the flight. I clearly resided in the presence of an extraordinary man, the CEO of the Six Flags operation.

Many days Hilda would just appear at the nursery with the same look of adoration. I conscientiously checked to see if anyone noticed. Somehow the physical relationship continued through this entire time. Maybe she came into town early or late afternoon if a builder's job was not scheduled. Maybe she came by during lunch if I could get away for a few minutes. She ran by at night sometimes after working late at her office. She was driven and consequently drove me.

Whether or not I could afford to hire another person, I brought in Jeannie as a part-time employee. After she was hired, Hilda came by and wisped me away for lunch, only lunch was usually secondary. She knew the town very well including out of the way private places. Her passion did not wane. I wondered if Jeannie suspected anything unusual. Surely she perceived Hilda's controlling hand over me.

One morning Hilda arrived early at the nursery, near opening time. We walked to the door between the greenhouse and the office. She pulled me in and kissed me passionately as Mr. Briggs opened the back door to the greenhouse. Looking startled, he quickly turned around and left. My embarrassment was beyond compare for I saw him or his wife almost daily. He had already been calling Hilda "that Burkshire woman." In fact, he had called my dad to report her frequent visits. If my parents ever suspected anything, they kept their silence.

Hilda continued driving into the nursery's gravel parking area with impromptu lunch plans. After she told Jeannie, off we'd go with her ideas. Ben's in Atlanta, a twenty-five minute trip, topped her list of favorite restaurants. My mouth waters even now remembering the taste of the fresh, perfectly fried shrimp. Since I hadn't really tasted shrimp that often, and certainly not while growing up, these lunches exceeded any other noontime meals I'd ever experienced.

Hilda asked if I wanted spumoni ice cream for dessert. What kind of ice cream was that? I learned soon as I savored every bite of that beyond delicious Italian treat. Other lunches consisted of fast food in Austell with a quick side trip for whatever she had in mind.

At any time of the day during business hours or after, I might turn around from my task to see her watching me with eyes of adoration. Conveniently located on the nursery proper, my house trailer provided moments of privacy.

Of course, returning to work as nonchalantly as possible, I felt guilty for any time away from business. Seemingly extremely adamant about my business venture, Hilda never minded taking me away. With an all-encompassing business dependent on horticultural knowledge, my presence was critical.

I often wondered how she managed to see me so frequently. I wondered if she ever saw her children. I didn't think she cared much about seeing Donald. She married at age 32 to a country bumpkin about four years younger. Had she married just to have children? Had she married to look normal in the eyes of the church? How could he hang around the house without contributing monetarily? Many questions played through my mind about their relationship. With Hilda clearly in charge, I suppose she needed this sort of man.

How I continued running that nursery, installing a growing amount of landscape jobs, dabbling at bookkeeping, and finding time for an illicit relationship, overwhelms me now. Our affair grew into an obsession. My demanding responsibilities paled in comparison to my need for her presence. I felt incomplete without her. She absorbed me. She compelled me to seek her companionship. She gave gifts.

Chapter 10

Camp Diversion

At a point during the early spring, I drove to her church camp on the east side of Atlanta. Actually, she and her parents and sisters help establish the camp and served an integral part in its operation. She thought the new pine trees needed fertilizing on the acreage and wanted my opinion. We walked over the property, and I concurred with the need for fertilization. On the concrete floor of the ladies' camp style bathroom, I suppose she found something to lay on the concrete. We made love right there at the church camp.

The trees were fertilized at a later time using a small diameter post hole digger to drill a few holes around the drip line of each tree. A specified amount of fertilizer was poured into each hole, covered over with the dug up soil, and watered.

Chapter 11

Back to Business

After a year or so, I began having a continuous headache. Aspirin, the only medication for headaches to my knowledge, became my constant companion. I took so many aspirins each day; the amount had to exceed the suggested dosage. My head pounded with each bump the road inflicted on me as I drove my pick up.

By now I had the good fortune of learning about landscape design from two men, who were partners in the landscape architecture business. I wish I could remember how we met. At any rate, I drove to their office in Atlanta occasionally to learn the fundamentals about landscape architecture. Though I commanded a reliable knowledge of horticulture, I had not taken any design courses. These unselfish men opened new opportunities for me that I didn't realize until later. They contracted me to place large boulders for a residential landscaping job. The house looked like a sprawling mansion with a huge front yard.

Obviously I possessed potential in the field of horticulture, but I was wearing down. The nagging headache reared itself again. I was driven toward a goal of success recognizing the obligation to my parents, but I was also driven by the compelling obsession that never left me. Hilda ruled my world. She consumed me like a fire consumes wood and leaves it in ashes.

Hilda wanted a prayer garden for the church, so I roughed out a design on the spot, which resulted in a bold kiss on location. Later working with some young people from the church, we created a prayer garden relying on the existing oak trees as the fundamental landscape and adding some plant material and a concrete bench or two. The completion of this project brought praise for both of us.

At least one day a week, Hilda whisked me away for lunch. Even though I mentioned this once before, I want to further elaborate. She told my dear, dependable Jeannie, she was taking me to lunch. Often these lunches evolved into elongated lunch times as one of her favorite spots was located in Atlanta. The superb shrimp won my taste buds alone with a dessert completely new to me - spumoni ice cream.

Because of Hilda's charisma and gift of gab, Jeannie never voiced a protest to me about these times away from the nursery. Other lunches bought nearer the nursery often ended somewhere on the edge of town for some kissing at least. Any amount of time lost from work hit me at some point. Watering plants after dark because of an impending freeze alert stressed me and added to my tiredness. Creating a landscape plan and a tangible list for a builder's job, or trying to sort out bookkeeping, which was not my forte, always happened after hours.

In the midst of this merry-go-round, I traded in my college Dart for a 1964 Volkswagen bug and the Brigg's old faithful three-quarter ton 50's model flatbed truck for a 390 cubic inch Chevy pick-up. That brought some unfavorable remarks from my property owners. I had bought the business but leased the land. And, their concern proved well founded as the one-half ton capacity diminished the amount of weight I could carry when delivering St. Augustine grass or shrubs to customers. I looked good in that red and white fashionable Chevy pick-up, but I also have snippets of memories with my head pounding as I drove to a landscape appointment after business hours.

Before I stupidly traded in the three quarter ton truck, it served as my major work horse, customized with a hydraulic lift. However, my employee Amberto loved driving the Chevy pick up to deliver sod, soil, and shrubs in Austell and nearby towns. My favorite experience happened with the Chevy one and one-half ton truck I owned as well. A buying trip to East Texas wholesale nurseries to buy merchandise for spring business became my responsibility. The Briggs insisted this trip carried a successful tradition forward, that the lower prices for plant material made the trip worthwhile, and I could hand pick the merchandise. Nursery wholesalers in the Tyler area claimed a brisk part of Georgia business with their acres of container shrubs and plant material ready for digging. I bought a truck load of cherry laurel, wax leaf ligustrum, various euonymus varieties, Japanese boxwood, yaupon holly, azaleas, and other plants suitable for cultivation in the Atlanta area.

Strong men weren't standing by when I arrived at the nursery with a truck load of plant or had a load delivered. The unloading personel consisted of Amberto and me, but sometimes just me. Specified locations for each plant type organized underneath lattice work kept an overall neat look. Balled and burlapped shrubs and small trees were set in saw dust to keep in the moisture. Water spigots with hoses at-tached, scattered throughout the display area, were critical to the time consuming process of watering plant material. A few times I thought I would freeze myself as I watered plants because a freeze warning alert was issued.

I find myself elaborating these details trying to emphasize the perpetual busy nature of running a business and the heavy responsibilities in every area associated with the business. My thoughts of Hilda counseling me in everyday business practices soon vanished. She acted as my "rah-rah" team all rolled into one person. Whether or not she held a clue about the nursery and landscaping business didn't keep her from fueling me with high expectations and telling others of my attributes. If Hilda were not present physically at the nursery, she was present en absentee. Her unending, constant attention engulfed and surrounded me further stretching my physical and emotional capacity to a thin covering, which eventually stretched too tightly.

Chapter 12

Physical Crisis

One Saturday morning a couple of years after I began the nursery business, I could not get up. I mean I could not get up from my bed. Luckily, I kept a phone on the floor within my reach. Saturdays are notoriously busy days in the plant nursery world. I called Jeannie and told her the problem. She had developed into a dependable and loyal employee and told me not to worry. Then I dialed Hilda. She somehow propelled me to her car and drove me to a doctor's office. He examined me and did blood work. I waited at Hilda's friend's home for the results. The report confirmed an acute case of mononucleosis.

Working beyond my capabilities caught up with me. My mother and one of my sisters traveled to Austell with the idea of transferring me to my hometown hospital. Almost as soon as the car movement began, I threw up. Any motion caused vomiting. Mother returned to Austell, and thanks to the generous heart of a church member, I flew home in a private plane. I still threw up, but the travel time was cut significantly. Of course, Hilda flew with me. I'm sure she had her hands full on that flight.

We landed at our small hometown airstrip, which usually only handled spray planes used for cotton defoliation. Quickly settled into a hospital room with an IV dripping away, nothing mattered except my wanting Hilda near me.

Thoughts about my nursery business responsibilities paled in comparison to the thought of separation. After being totally consumed by her for two years, I despaired at her leaving but needed to hide those feelings.

Even after my release from the hospital, bed rest was ordered. I didn't even walk to the restroom on my own. My dad carried me to the commode and back to bed. Hilda called me every other day or so, but we had no privacy. With one central corded phone in the kitchen, everybody heard everybody's conversations. I had grown accustomed to my own place and my own privacy. Especially Mother was leery of Hilda's calls. She had not treated Hilda in a friendly manner at all. At first I couldn't leave the bedroom anyway to call her, and even if I had called, the number would show on my par-ents' long distance bill. I knew that idea was not smart.

How my dad handled the nursery busi-ness situation I don't know. He managed to unearth the lease and paid off the bank. I'm sure his organizational skills, his people skills, and his expeditious mindset were core in the disbursal of this business. He paid $2,500.00 to the Austell bank and said he would just subtract that money from my inheritance. Of course, that never happened.

I've often wondered how the nursery business would have played out for me without Hilda's influence. The Atlanta newspaper wrote a lengthy article about me with pictures. Accolades were common. Customers admired my drive and my young age as a business owner. My two full-time employees respected me, and church kids wanted to work at the nursery.

What if I had run that business unen-cumbered? The founding of a business without business education or experience called for trouble. I thoroughly understand that. Perhaps with a different mind set, I would have never ventured into that large of an operation. I would hope if I had "gone for it," so to speak, I would have had the good sense to seek business guidance. I can deliberate on the "what if's" at length and dream about my unfulfilled accomplishments.

Chapter 13

Recovery and Return

My parents must have cringed at the thought of my returning to Austell after three months recuperation. I had no alternative plan other than to return. Even with my loving parents and sister supporting my time of healing, my desire to return grew every day. After all, the mobile home sat in Austell filled with my worldly possessions. I'm sure Dad arranged for its removal from the nursery property, and I'm sure Hilda found the trailer park a block or two behind her office.

Back in Austell, what was I to do? I tired easily from my acute bout with mono, so I knew I couldn't last very long at any task. Hilda's all-consuming care took over and afforded me further time to rest. As a prominent figure from a prominent family in the fundamental church, she played a major role in the planning and operation of their church's singing camp each summer. I mentioned this camp earlier. My recuperation continued in Hilda's special tent on campgrounds. With no expectations of any kind, I participated seldom, which suited me physically at that time.

A marriage announcement between my cousin and Hilda's niece necessitated a trip to Indiana. No question, I would travel with Hilda and her family in their family station wagon, which Hilda had bought no thanks to her non-working husband. The back seat folded down to create a space long enough to lie down. Since the plan was to travel straight through, this made resting possible for rotating drivers. After two or three hours of travel, Hilda moved her son Keith to the passenger's seat she had vacated and laid down in the back between Ruth and me. In a matter on minutes, she began cupping my breast underneath my bra. Arousing me, she ventured further into intimacy. I feared being noticed, but she didn't seem to worry. Soon she moved her hand to my private area stroking my clitoris with me still being solicitous about making a sound and consequently being discovered by her husband or someone else in the car. I did come. Apparently, no one noticed. Wow! I thought that particular action very nervy on Hilda's part but no more nervy than other events.

We stopped for gasoline a few hours into the trip, and the two of us walked to the ladies' restroom. Hilda closed the door and slammed me against it kissing me passionately. I suppose she never thought about the top panel of the door being glass. Although it wasn't clear glass, wavy figures were distinguishable. When we returned to the car, her husband harsh-ly whispered but loud enough for me to hear, "I've never seen such a passionate kiss in my life. I was never so embarrassed, and the service station guy saw it, too."

Like I was gripped in a vice by the unsettling scene, I move mechanically and without a word as I entered the car. How Hilda coped with her husband, I don't know except that I don't believe they spoke to each other throughout the trip unless absolutely necessary. I tried to keep a low profile around him. Other than internalizing that feeling, the remainder of the car trip remains a total blur.

My aunt greeted us joyfully as we arrived near the screened back door of her white, two-story wood home. Their 1965 Chevrolet Impala in a large detached garage spurred home memories. Here she stood, so animated, so full of vitality, so lovable. Hilda's best friend, my aunt, hugged me affectionately while I tried to act normally wishing myself invisible to Donald.

Soon my Uncle David appeared relieving me of immediate attention.

Because both women owned the gift of loquacity, chatter persisted through supper and into the evening. Eventually, discussion about the <u>Bible</u> monopolized the conversation. With these people I had learned to expect long and detailed Biblical insightful discussions. Uncle David, a preacher defending the doctrine of predestination, my aunt a devoted convert, and Hilda's lifetime experience in this doctrine, articulate opinions and expositions filled the room. Donald rarely contributed. Surely I talked a bit but the three carried the conversation.

Not soon enough I retired to my upstairs bedroom. Antique furniture filled every room with warmth and Indiana personality. Hardwood floors creaked occasionally as I moved around preparing for bed. "What was it like in Hilda and Donald's bedroom after today's scary event?" I asked myself. However, while speculating about their conversation, my door opened. Hilda approached me in that same unique passionate manner. She said, "I'll come by and get you in the morning."

I dressed quickly in Levi's and t-shirt after being awakened early. We crept down the dark wood stairway, out a side door, and walked finally into a corn field. What direction or whose cornfield I have no idea. She unzipped my jeans and began caressing my genitalia, then my clitoris. She pressed the back of my body against the front of hers as in a passion filled cocoon. Surely the events of the day before and the chances involved in this clandestine venture predicted my failure to climax. Nevertheless, she demonstrated her insatiable appetite for me by taking further chances for intimate contact.

Totally enveloped in seven foot corn stalks, we walked until the horizon appeared bathed in its early morning red light. We immediately saw a farm house and somehow knew they attended the same church as my aunt and uncle. Maybe Hilda had mapped out the route. I don't doubt her capacity for doing so. I felt apprehension when we stepped upon the wood porch, but I knew Hilda could handle any situation with that gift of gab. Not surprisingly, Mrs. Crawford invited us inside. Hilda used the magic word Thomas.

We were guest of Elder David and Ruth. We were ushered into the kitchen where the smells of bacon, eggs, and biscuits mingled together and fused into a welcomed interlude for my thoughts. I wasn't even distracted when Mrs. Crawford called Aunt Ruth to notify her of our whereabouts. Aunt Ruth appeared shortly as her usual vivacious self. She made light of our early morning walk. Thank goodness!

However, my aunt's relationship with Hilda lead to deeper confusion inside me. What exactly was her relationship with Hilda? Had they shared sexual events? Acting "normal" throughout our visit proved tedious as I played with scenarios about Hilda and my aunt, or Hilda and Donald's interactions, or about my interactions with Donald. My best option obviously was avoidance. The car trip back to Austell fades in memory.

I had no job, but I worked at length to stay near Hilda. Being away from her was unfathomable. With previous landscaping connections, I installed a few jobs with the aide of Amberto and friends. One of the jobs I bid necessitated working with a church committee. I learned a lesson. Don't ever work with a committee expecting a decision. I spent so much time for nothing. My heart stayed in the nursery and landscaping business, but without a full time crew of laborers and without my former physical stamina, I faltered.

Chapter 14

The Real Estate Business

      Hilda came to my rescue offering me a job at her office plus fees to cover real estate school. Back and forth to Atlanta I drove for weeks to master the required courses for being a real estate agent. I passed the test and obtained my license within a few weeks. The learning material interested me somewhat, but I resolved to study hard and pass the test for Hilda. My duties mainly consisted of researching property at the county court house and gathering information about tracts of land. Leg work and research afforded me a comfort zone with the business. The classic real estate business, showing houses, did not click with me. The tracts of land Hilda had listed interested me perhaps because of my farm kid background. Photographing aerial views of acreage brought reward by utilizing my photography skills. Flying in a private plane to photograph tracts of land highlighted my real estate days.

Chapter 15

Marriage

A really amazing event happened during this time. I married. At twenty-five, didn't I need to marry? I loved Kurt and felt a powerful attraction for him, but my emotions had not recovered enough from the Hilda filled days. I met this good-looking young man at the church camp. I felt his attraction toward me, and I was attracted to him. I loved the attention from him but harbored a fear about it at the same time.

My parents spent the usual money parents spend on a daughter's wedding. Invitations, showers, dresses, flowers, music, and so many details were handled long distance. The promise of sainthood would pale in comparison to my parent's love and support toward me. They knew little about the young man, but they financed a wedding taking place in the Fellowship Church, of which they had no connection. Unselfishly, they chose hope for the future over doubt.

The future lasted about six months. I couldn't stand sex. Unfortunately, or so I thought at the time, I confessed my illicit relationship with Hilda to Kurt before we married. According to him after consulting with his doctor, women didn't like sex with men after experiencing it with a woman.

However, I did try other stereotyped ideas of marriage by attempting to cook. Through my years at home, my mother modeled cooking to the fullest extent of the word. However, I had little experience with cooking since my high school days. But, I do remember preparing meals using a cookbook entitled "Meals for Two." Surely I cleaned the house and washed some clothes as well.

My cooking efforts soon fizzled as I kept dinner warm for nothing. Kurt wasn't hungry when he arrived home late from work. Some friends finally invited me to their home and hit me with the news. I was living with an unfaithful husband. Could I blame him? A young, healthy red-blooded American boy had needs. This young man had positive expectations for a happy marriage. These people knew nothing of my secret life, but it plagued me as I thought about how that life had impacted both Kurt and me. But, on the instructions of my psychiatrist Dr. Saul, the marriage soon ended. Hilda arranged a session with this lady psychiatrist because of my distraught condition. Hilda set up the whole sorted mess that ended in a regrettable traumatic experience for Kurt and one that taints my life to this day. After two sessions, the doctor told me to throw him out and change the locks. Under the spell of the devil incarnate, I did the deed. That afternoon Kurt came home, couldn't get in, called my name, banged on the door, picked up his belongings and left. I didn't see him again for forty-four years. How he pulled himself up from that incomprehensible blow, I don't know. I tried to move on but guilt accompanied me to the core.

Now, my turn for a complete deceptive pounding arrived at my next doctor's appointment. Did I do what she said to do? Did I put his belongings in the yard and change the locks? Yes. She proceeded to bombard me calling me a terrible, selfish person. She chewed me up and spit me out. She stomped on me and left me flat and useless. Did I respond or counter her words? I don't remember. I sat in a state of shock. Somehow I felt Hilda called the shots and orchestrated this entire scenario. After all, she could talk herself into anything or out of anything as a master manipulator. I drove away from Atlanta understanding the phrase "feeling lower than a snake." I didn't regret his leaving at the time because of the freedom from sex with a man. Seemingly, the emotions wrapped around Hilda gave me little room for other emotions. But, then, my life equalled emotion; emotion equalled life. The bombarding realization of the devastating blow to a young man's life, the demoralizing attack on me from a professional psychiatrist, and the encroaching thoughts of deception Hilda orchestrated, played together in my mind. I regretted my treatment toward another human being plus the many other peripheral consequences. Not one thank you card did I write for all the thoughtful wedding gifts. My unhappiness outweighed my etiquette. I know my parents dismayed over that social blunder. My self-esteem suffered from the attack of a supposed professional person. My psyche couldn't cope with the idea of Hilda's deception. With my physical body not up to par since the acute case of mononucleosis, and the constant emotional issues plaguing my mind, my "self" ebbed toward a fragile state of existence.

Chapter 16

The Showdown

More time on my hands allowed more thought to real estate but also more time with Hilda, despite a lingering trace of mistrust. Lord have mercy. I should have been away from her. But yet again, it became unbearable to spend time away from her. Her husband had no clue of my presence some evenings in their home. They communicated very little anyway. Even without the physical factor, I was trapped emo-tionally. I can offer no logical explanation for that shroud, that absorption and utter obsession for another person.

Living through this unsettling conflict preoccupied my days and my nights. Being with anyone else except her only brought loneliness. Loneliness prevailed and overtook me when deprived of her presence.

She left me in charge of the real estate office while she and her family took a vacation. This event signified their very first vacation as a family. Those poor kids didn't know what they had missed through the years. Hilda's actions of late included more time with her children. I'm sure they had never known life with her around, but she gained ground with two kids hungering for their mother's attention.

Her husband had even secured a job but drove by the office all the time. However, I perceived her efforts to appease him. All these factors played into the idea and initiation of a family vacation.

In my obsessed mind, an idea formed in my brain. This responsibility of running the office created a perfect chance for me to demonstrate my real estate education and training. I had researched a property south of Atlanta before she contacted the owner and succeeded in listing the forty or so acres. A brain flash hit me. <u>Time Magazine</u> interviewed and published an article about an Atlanta millionaire. I had recently read the article. The fact that he supported Boy Scouts generously, and had been a Boy Scout himself, impressed me. My brain flash rushed full force into the idea of this wealthy gentleman purchasing the forty acres as a gift to the Boy Scouts. With large live oak trees covering a rolling terrain, and a creek meandering through the property, what better setting for camping and hiking by excited Boy Scouts?

I developed a portfolio specifically for the business magnet. Already talented with organizational skills, I prepared the packet to the best of my knowledge and ability. My appointment was secured, not with the man himself, but with his sister. At least that gave me entry into the downtown Dallas building and a hearing with his right-hand assistant.

The afternoon I walked into Ms. Davis' office, I was determined not to show nerves. I was determined to present my idea using the portfolio's organizational flow. She received me graciously in her expansive, white office. Everything was white. White furniture and white carpeting saturated with light from a window overlooking Atlanta, filled me with awe. Of course, she didn't commit but retained the portfolio I offered. She would speak with her brother and call me.

I left that office on a high thinking job well done. After all, I had the brain flash, secured the appointment, created a professional looking portfolio, and presented my original idea to a top-ranking officer in the business world. Originality and ingenuity I claimed for myself.

Hilda was furious. No other word adequately explains her reaction to my run at pleasing her with my business prowess. I was shocked. No other word adequately explains my reaction. "Don't you ever do anything like that again without consulting me!" she yelled. I know I sat in stunned silence while she ranted at me. As the picture came together, I felt hurt, berated for my unselfish motive to build business, and betrayed by her superficial confidence in me. With the massive amount of energy erupting, I lashed out verbally in defense of my actions as anger grabbed me. She said something about my leaving. I didn't intend to leave the premises. Hilda left in her car.

I sat at my desk in a daze, stunned at her reaction. In a quandary about what I should do, yet not understanding what I had done wrong, I thought my actions had demonstrated ingenuity, creativity, and follow through. Surely we could work it out. What I had so proudly performed wasn't wrong. I just sat at my desk deep in thought. Who could I call for an opinion? She was my person to call, my confidante. She was my closest friend.

Some time later, the front office door opened. Usually conscience of time, I hadn't conscientiously thought about time.

My mind was sorting through my supposed horrible offense and trying to fathom the idea of alienation from Hilda. My emotions were not ready for that prospect. Into the location of my office walked Hilda followed by her two kids, then about thirteen and fourteen. She asked me to leave adding the embarrassment of her children's presence. A scuffle began between us, nothing like a women's wrestling match, but a scuffle. She moved into the office entry room with us engaged in some sort of physical entan-glement. I remember her kids watching. How dare she bring her children! The door sprang open, and two policemen rushed in. They ad-vanced on me without hesitation, using some sort of spray and forcing me into a strait jacket. Later I realized a call to the police had been placed before she ever entered the building. I could imagine her using that articulate ver-biage to describe me as a threat to her safety.

The reality of a strait jacket sank in. How humiliating. How unfair. Tear gas is an ungodly sting to the eyes. At least I retained enough gumption not to fight against the confinement. The idea of tear gas and a strait jacket left me utterly devastated. This moment changed my life. I had been deceived, humiliated, and knocked down by a desperate woman. But, I was not broken. That glimmer of "self" stayed with me as the police car drove into the night. Were they taking me to jail? I had no idea and no inclination to ask. I stayed silent. They finally stopped and escorted me into a large building. No communication ensued. The light dawned when the elevator door opened and bright lights hit my eyes. They were giving information to someone at a nurse's station. Some man in a white coat helped me into a room where other people sat on the floor. Even as upset and unhappy as I felt, I knew exactly where the police had brought me.

At some point the strait jacket was removed. I'm uncertain whether I sat in a chair or on the floor. One certainty grabbed me, I was in the "loony bin!" The infamous 7th Floor. Perhaps they (the staff) pictured me as out of control because of the strait jacket, but I was very much in control. I watched a lady sitting on the floor rocking back and forth just like in the movies. Another lady yelled out periodically. A couple of other ladies sat quietly in this very stark white thirty by thirty space. Early on I knew my mother was coming to get me out the next day, but I don't remember talking with her.

Someone else talked with her for sure; I'll describe that momentarily. Since family rescue was imminent, I tried to relax as much as one can in that situation. Yes, I could relax surrounded by ladies with mental issues and staff dressed in white treating me like one of the patients. Maybe because they gave me a shot of something. One can guess the contents in the syringe. At least I dozed off to "la-la" land knowing my relief was forthcoming. That gave me hope. Hilda called my mother and told her what she had done. That she had essentially committed me. Of course, Mother was given the hospital name in Atlanta. Hilda asked Mother if she could do anything, to which my mother replied, "I think you've done quite enough." Way to go, Mother!

The next morning I was escorted to the resident psychiatrist's office. He wanted me to relate the reason for my placement on the 7th floor. I know he was just doing his job, as they say, but with the medication mostly gone from my system, my thinking cleared. I told him I didn't intend to tell him anything because it was too involved, and that my family would be there soon to get me released. He was extremely unhappy about my stance, but he could tell I wasn't going to budge.

One of the greatest reliefs of my life happened that day when I was released from that place. Talk about depressing. I tried my best to entertain positive thoughts, but that was a tremendous expectation. After all, the person I had loved, the person I thought loved me had committed me. She had to save face. Not only did my mother appear on that floor of humiliation, but my teacher sister and the family pastor Bro. Strickland volunteered his time to help me. Travel time alone took a couple of hours. I couldn't believe my eyes as I grasped the support provided me by my family and their pastor. That moment of support began triggering reality into my life once more. Who really cared for me and about me? Betrayal is an emotional bomb waiting to explode. When I reflect back to the unbelievable office incident, I know my pain, my panic of loosing this person, and my fear of the future all erupted from that one word. Betrayal. Betrayal's wrath kills the spirit. Only God can dispel and sweep away a destructive spirit.

Chapter 17

Survival

I reclaimed the church denomination of my first twenty-one years and even began forming a musical group of young people. The pastor trusted me. That trust surprised and strengthened me. God's plan unfolded like a well-written lesson plan. A talented and unusually moti-vated group of teens teamed with me to form a group using electric guitars, acoustic guitars, a keyboard, a drum, and singers. We sang in the home church, we performed at an outdoor community event, at a church encampment, and made a trip to Atlanta to sing in a couple of churches. I lucked into the perfect music for this group, and they bought into it full force. Singing about Jesus served to mature their faith and restore my faith. Now in their fifties, these teenagers of the past still remember their music group experience with fondness. My self-confidence and faith increased watching these teenagers blossom individually and unify as a group. My healing began but strained to reach complete attainment.

Finding another means of support permeated my waking thoughts. I couldn't continue living with my parents remaining financially dependent on them. As the daughter of a WWII vet, I'd been exposed to stories of Army life, particularly about Australia and New Guinea. With a college degree in my pocket, I could enter Officer Training School if accepted by a branch of the service. Paper work accomplished, the Navy contacted me first. They flew me to Albuquerque, New Mexico, for an interview. The recruiting officer toured me around the base but mostly introduced me to the social side of Navy life. I think he enjoyed interviewing women to entertain women. The Army's interview was conducted by a friendly but all business female. By the time the red tape stopped rolling, I had already accepted a job in Athens. The notification of acceptance into the Army's OTC program came too late. Perhaps I should have dropped the new job to snatch this opportunity. How do we ever know for sure?

Chapter 18

Moving On

As much as I appreciated the support of family and loved the singing youth group, I'd lived independently, owned a business, and met Mr. Responsibility head on. Time marched forward regardless of my situation. I had to move on. Through a job advertisement ad in the Athens, Georgia, newspaper, I applied, interviewed, and succeeded in securing a job. This job took me into a completely different career opportunity. Interestingly, my horticulture knowledge fit the job description but from a different perspective. I worked with mentally or emotionally challenged kids training them in a greenhouse setting. We potted marigolds and watched them grow. We planted zinnia seeds and watched them sprout. Most of these kids had passed "kid age;" however, they reacted excitedly like children and hugged their teachers like kindergartners. Two unexpected friendships developed between the current staff and me. We planned together to improve their horticulture experience even finding lawn maintenance jobs for guys appropriate for the task. Several local businesses cooperated in this work program for the mentally challenged.

My personal job history repeated itself in an uncanny way. I received a call from Doris Linley inviting me to the position of landscape designer in her recently acquired nursery in Atlanta. Historically and successfully known as Baker Brother's, they retired and placed the business for sale. Doris declared, "I thought of you immediately." Her husband owned a popular shop inside the Six Flags Over Georgia park giving him first-hand knowledge of the plant labeling project I successfully completed. Actually, the first time I met Clint, Hilda introduced me. Their acquaintance sprang from a past real estate transaction. Clint and Doris had already became customers of mine purchasing plants from my Austell nursery business. The repetition in my history surprised me. Two or three days after Doris' call and before I formally placed a letter of resignation to the state school in Athens, I was offered a department head job with a pay raise, of course. Unbelievable! The same scenario slammed me again. I opted for the Atlanta job. Obviously, concerns rose about this location and its close proximity to Hilda. Could I handle the hurtful memories thrust upon me? Could I let "by-gones be by-gones" and not contact her in anyway? The idea of full time landscape design and installation supervision sparked my interest. I enjoyed an amiable relationship with Doris and Clint.

By the time I arrived on the job, Doris had recreated the typical nursery style office into a tastefully decorated gift shop. A well-planned design room and office was located away from customer flow providing a workspace free of interruptions. And, to the advantage of both nursery sales and future landscaping, the orig-inal work force remained intact. Their knowledge and experience contributed daily to the overall operation.

My new work situation held promise and excitement. However, that nagging, unrelenting tug of war pulled me over the line, then back again. For some illogical reason, I secured an apartment in Austell instead of Atlanta. Life flowed along in a stable manner mainly because one of my sisters lived with me for the summer as she attended college and worked at Six Flags Over Georgia. Because of a rewarding job and my sister's visit, time progressed with days filled by activities and companionship.

With her summer semester and summer job finished, Lynn returned to Athens for fall semester. That's exactly when problems crept back. Now, I had extra time after the work day and extra time to think. "Well, it wouldn't hurt to make contact," thoughts ran through my head. How could I entertain such a stupid idea after absolute deception?

I did, in fact, contact her without mentioning the episode. She did, in fact, appear at the nursery a few times. I felt uncomfortable when she visited but wanted her presence nonetheless. I can't even fathom myself, other than the hold on me that coiled like a snake loosening then constricting but never quite slithering away.

Other than a few times at the nursery, we did not see each other. I suppose I grieved over the loss. A person, a personality, had completely saturated my being, then extracted herself through deceit. Why would I seek the presence of this person? The relationship had taken such an abrupt turn, I couldn't grasp its ending. No closure happened, no situation freed me to move on.

Chapter 19

Almost Fatal

Even the ideal job didn't assuage my pain. I became more and more depressed without fully understanding I was depressed. That doesn't make sense, but that's my best explanation. Facing another night of unhappiness in my efficiency apartment, I decided to take several sleeping pills and end my increasingly empty life. Late in the evening, I took several pills believing I had finished my life. Loud telephone rings punctured the thick fog in my brain. Though heavy with sleep and fuzzy in thought, I answered the phone. Doris' voice sounded through the ear piece after my slurring hello. In her typical Southern drawl, she said, "You didn't come in to work; I felt I needed to check on you." From the almost incoherent sound of my voice, a red flag waved in Doris' mind. Doris said she was going to call me every fifthteen minutes. Through her persistency, I reveled to full consciousness after whatever time passed. I credit Doris with saving my life. My life had been spared two other times. I totaled the brand new family car during the Christmas holidays my first year of college. People remarked they didn't see how anyone could have survived that wreck. The Christmas holidays of the following year, I was doomed again. My sister and I lounged in bed as the new central heating system released gas fumes back into the house. We were the only ones affected because others were up and moving around. We both passed out when we came in contact with fresh air. A Nigerian couple spending Christmas with us recognized what had happened and saved our lives. Both were medically trained. My sister and I spent many hours under oxygen tents. A cat has nine lives they say. I'd spent three of mine by age twenty-seven.

Doris and I shared a long conversation the next day. For the first time, and very few times since, I related the story of Hilda. Remember they were acquaintances, Doris did not consid-er herself a friend. Doris deserved some expla-nation. She felt a definite pull to call me that morning. I related my story about Hilda to her.

Even with the hope of a nonjudicial attitude, the embarrassment of divulging a secret of that magnitude was a gigantic step. I'll never forget what she said as we ended our conversation, "A love is a love." One of my fears hinged on Doris taking a condemning spirit stance, but a spirit of understanding replaced my fear.

With that traumatic experience behind me and with Doris' supportive, nonjudgmental friendship encouraging me, I moved on to replace Hilda. Somehow I had to physically, emo-tionally, and spiritually replace my obsession of this person undeserving of my obsession. Physically, I moved to Atlanta near my work. Emotionally and spiritually, I joined a church, sang in the choir, and made new friends who invited me to Sunday lunch and other activities like theatrical productions. I continued contact with one special couple for many years. Doris and Clint continued their unwavering support even including me in some social events. Importantly, I began contacting my family more often. My youngest sister and her boyfriend visited me taking advantage of the apartment swimming pool. That time together remains a highlight to this day.

Chapter 20

Second Marriage

One afternoon as I, almost happily, created a landscape design, Doris brought a young man into my office introducing him as a past employee of the original Baker's Bros. Nursery. He had attended the University of Georgia as well, had lived on a farm near a small southern Georgia town, and displayed warmth and friendliness. As a landscape designer himself, we began discussing the plan in progress on my drafting table. Soon we began collaborating together easily and naturally. After work we enjoyed dinner and talked for hours on end. Common areas of interest and the basic farm life upbringing sparked a friendship. Conversation flowed. We enjoyed another evening together before he returned to his landscape design job in

Athens. Six months later we married. Surprise!

I had to redeem myself and remarry. Marriage and family as one was expected. My first attempt at marriage proved disastrous, but I so hoped for the best with Jack. Deep down in my soul I loved someone else and had loved him almost my entire life, but he had married years before. Another man I had loved stayed covered by my regretful past.

This man Jack did not "put the moves on me" so to speak. He acted like a perfect gentleman. My grandmothers loved him. We married in my uncle Howell's home where my musically talented sister Carol sang "The First Time Ever I Saw Your Face" more beautifully than Roberta Fleck.

By late afternoon we were welcomed by Jack's friends at an upscale home on the outskirts of Atlanta. Special for me, Doris and Clint awaited our arrival, also. We spent a happy, compatible evening with the two couples as Jack enjoyed his liquor with enthusiasm. In fact, his indulging resulted in a deep sleep. I thought a one time event on a special occasion was understandable. What I didn't know would hurt me. I soon lived with Jack's cycle of alcohol addiction. He worked at a local nursery in Athens most days. I later discovered he simply didn't show up other days. Sometimes he didn't show up at home either. Since I had never known the life of an alcoholic, I lacked knowledge in dealing with this overnight, life-changing situation. The word <u>binge</u> became part of my vocabulary and progressed into my reality.

After I met the nursery owners, they invited me to join the business as another landscape designer. Now, the same company employed Jack and me.

Surely the escapades would stop since we were working for the same company. Now here's the funny part. We drove separately to work because appointments took us to different homes and businesses. Some mornings Jack's car was squarely in my rear view mirror, then at next glance, no car. How had that happened? Schooled by my upbringing of acting responsibly, I ordered myself to work thinking his car would appear at any moment. Two or three days later arriving home after work, I'd find him on the floor of our second bedroom surrounded by beer cans and an overflowing ashtray nearby. I began calling this area his "nest." As one might guess, the unconsummated marriage drained me emotionally. I didn't even know I had enough emotional juices left to deal with another traumatic experience. After four or five months of this scenario, I traveled to the farm specifically to talk with Dad.

"At age thirty-two and never married, maybe he has to get used to being with a woman."

"A man doesn't have to get used to a woman!" Dad said between guffaws. Other than feeling really stupid and a bit hurt by all the laughter, a moment of full awakening happened. When the laughter faded, Dad began helping me with a plan of action.

Jack and I moved away from the Athens' cycle with the understanding he would attend Alcoholics Anonymous. I returned to my past position in Atlanta knowing I needed a stable income job. Jack assured me he could find landscaping business in the area. He did not attend AA's. He did not contribute financially to our household even though he supposedly drove to another landscaping nursery many times a week. Even though no money appeared, a draftsman did. I arrived home one day to find Jack's draftsman working on the structural part of a landscape project. This cute, friendly black guy had been hired as Jack's draftsman. The thought flashed through my mind, "OK. How is this possible? I haven't seen any money from Jack except in the form of a new sports coat for himself."

Not long after that day, I moved to my own apartment and filed for divorce. Annulments are more costly. When I rang the doorbell a couple of days after leaving, another guy answered the door. A new thought passed through my brain, "Well, that didn't take long," which coincided with asking if Jack were home. Thank goodness an old high school friend had accompanied me to gather my belongings.

Thank goodness for her support, and the communication we shared. The moment of reality happened when I knocked on that door.

Now, life. What? I'd been involved in an all-consuming relationship with a woman, married a guy whom I had treated poorly, and lived through a "so-called" marriage to a gay guy. I couldn't have conjured up such a life in my wildest imagination, nor would I wish for such a life. And, almost inconceivable, the deliberate sleeping pill incident preceded Jack's time with all those complications. I'm exhausted just remembering those seven years. Only God knows how I persisted through those times.

Being in closer contact with my family helped me remember their love and concern. I couldn't have asked for a better job and supportive employer. Friendships formed at church filled a need as well as a place to belong and a fulfilled the need to contribute to a worthy cause. The church became a touching point to renew my faith thus filtering strength into life's foundation as nurtured from childhood.

Chapter 21

Saddest Time in My Life

My boxes were still unpacked when my sister Carol and her husband came to visit. My advancement to overcome the past moved mostly forward, but sadness invaded my thoughts from time to time. Hence, the action of unpacking just hadn't happened. Nonetheless, they arrived and didn't make a big deal about the boxes.

I didn't realize the next day, Sunday, would be my last day to spend with my sister ever. Don, her husband, photographed us standing near a classic car just north of Six Flags. We toured the Wax Museum making jokes and reminiscing about events surrounding the life-like wax figures. Some didn't look so life-like.

Monday morning meant a workday beginning at eight o'clock. An hour or so later, Carol and Don had finished packing their car and came by the nursery for a final goodbye. That moment in time did mark a final goodbye. At age twenty-six, Carol died in a car accident the next morning after spending the night with another sister and her husband.

People comment often about "how I couldn't believe my ears." Well, I couldn't believe my ears. My dad informed me by phone. As gently as he tried to break the news, my heart instantly broke from pain. My fist slammed the drafting table breaking my watch crystal. This one instance in time defined and defines my moment of greatest sorrow. Only eighteen months stretched between our birth dates. My sister and my best friend was gone. Except to mention how Hilda fit into this tragedy, I won't dwell on details. Carol's story is another story.

The day dawned brightly promising its typical July heat. An after dawn light grew brighter as we drove toward another southern Georgia town, a town where many people knew my sister. Our immediate and extended families congregated in the home of my aunt and uncle. Talk and laughter and tears commingled together as kinfolks expressed their sorrows and offered their comforting words. Late morning I was called to the phone. "Hilda's on the phone," came the announcement from my aunt. Why did they talking stop, or seemingly so? I felt "showcased." I said little to her as she spoke the usual words one speaks to someone who has lost a loved one. My heart longed for the deep comfort I would have received at an earlier time, in another chapter of life. I hoped for a call; I hated the call. My mother's resentment for this person loomed over me rendering me less talkative than usual. Even if Mother did not suspect the full scope of the Hilda relationship, "the call" cinched my mother's growing dislike for this domineering woman.

Chapter 22

Back to Athens

So, off I venture into life again. My job beckoned me back. The reality of paying apartment rent and other living expenses forced me into play once more. A telephone call was funneled to me one afternoon while working at the nursery. On the line came a familiar voice. The owner of the Athens' nursery greeted me and chatted a couple of minutes before divulging the call's main purpose. "We'd like for you to return to Athens and work for us." Bang! There it was. Decision time again.

Two marriages broken that resulted in an unresolved relationship in the first and an odd, unforeseen relationship in the second. I had to "keep" myself. The least thought given these unsuccessful relationships became my guard against depression and degradation of self. I sprang headlong into my landscaping career in Athens and became actively involved in church activities eventually working with the youth group. Navigating toward the youth group was natural.

Before I bought a decent house in a blue-collar neighborhood, I lived in three funky places. Bless my mother and dad. They helped move me back to Athens. We searched for a rental, found one, and spent one night. My dad said, "We're not spending another night here." Airplanes flew overhead all night. And, I do mean all night. So, after a sleepless night, we returned to the real estate company for new suggestions. The next property was a weird little place practically in the center of an intersection, but it was new and clean. I lived there a few months until the goofy location got to me. Traffic moved on all sides of this little brick building. Who would build a rental on an asphalt island? Looking for something really different, I found it. Back in the cherry laurals on sandy soil and off the beat-en path sat a mobile home for sale. I bought it. Now, I had peace and quiet. That became a problem, though. Too much peace and quiet equaled loneliness. After a few months I had to leave. Luckily, the folks holding the paper, simply released me from the agreement. Was I ever relieved. Finally, my smart button depressed and I bought the house I described earlier. I planned to rent a room to help pay the mortgage payment. My two different renters were a mixed blessing. The extra money I liked; certain problems with a party girl I didn't like. I knew the risk of bringing another person into my residence. The next renter's stay was a positive experience. At least, I maintained the semblance of stability. I even bought a used lawn mower for the thick San Augustine grass. A detached garage housed my new Buick, and I had space to park the El Camino I drove for landscaping work.

Relating all these moves and thinking of the work involved with moving, I marvel at how I managed to succeed at my job. My job at the Athens' Nursery consisted of consulting with homeowners about their landscape needs, designing the landscaping, working up an es-timate, presenting it for approval, gathering the plant material and other materials for the job, and supervising the installation. In fact, I estimated one job for a bid opening through the company and was awarded the bid. To my knowledge, this job was the largest landscape job ever completed in Athens at the time. I ran three landscaping crews for six months. A few months later I lead a 10-man crew to the northern Georgia where we landscaped a parking lot for a large non denominational church. Landscaping a parking lot might not sound exciting, but the job was a challenge. During my stay in that area, I had dinner with three former Super Bowl champions. What team? That I don't remember, but I wish I did.

I considered the Mexican guys, who served as the crew, my friends. My designs meant nothing without them. We installed small front yard landscape jobs, a large tree here and there kind of jobs, as well as apartment complex landscape projects, and the other jobs I mentioned. Many Friday afternoons after work I met the men at the 7-11 Store and bought beer for them as a thank you.

Rewarding work and financial success ended at the Athens' Nursery when the owner made an X-rated remark to me. He wanted "in my pants," and I wanted out. That did it. I left. The dirty old man! I'd probably hit him where it hurts if that happened today.

Sex had become a problem in another way in my life. I haven't even mentioned the guys with the mentality of "You give me some; you'll get the job." I ran into these guys periodically and always in connection to business. Being a female in a male dominated field particularly had its challenges in the mid 1970's. Just as smoking remained an untouched issue back then, male promiscuity remained a given in the business world without a trace of change in the air. I came close to trouble one night on the lake after I had accepted an invitation from a con-tractor's son to drive along the lake. A little wine and a very aggressive young man made for an uncomfortable outing. "Am I going to get out of this?" certainly ran through my mind. Somehow I managed to avoid a sexual happening. I had already submitted a bid for the landscaping of a large apartment complex along the Interstate with this contractor's father. Surprise! I wasn't awarded the job.

The possibility of jobs awarded through the Minority Contractors' Organization presented prospective landscaping jobs, especially since the nursery owners were Hispanic. The director showed up uninvited to my home one evening. After some small talk and business related chatter, he showed his real reason for the visit. Another aggressive male thought he would use sex as a business bribe.

I encountered sexual innuendos throughout my landscaping career mainly because the field of work remained a male dominated world for many years. Another attitude some men projected dealt with capability. After winning one large landscaping bid presented in a room full of men, a loosing competitor remarked without fondness, "You'd better get busy." I knew that! Other men supported and encouraged me. My dad always told his daughters, "You can do anything you think you're big enough to do." The word <u>big</u> wasn't referring to physical size. By the way, I completed those large jobs successfully.

Chapter 23

Conclusion

Contacting my aunt's friend that summer day in 1967 changed the direction of my life. I am yet to understand how a person can monopolize another person's life to such an extreme measure. Sex played a huge part. It caused an emotional capture that erased logic and consequential thinking. Sex is sex in some cases. But, an all-consuming personality type can manipulate and bait a person through their charismatic personality coupled with sex. An all-consuming personality type absorbs the other person, so that he or she is no longer an entity but an extension of the other person. The depth of this extension is adjustable at the whelm of the perpetrator.

A perpetrator in the greatest sense of the word not only abuses sexually but mentally, emotionally, and spiritually. This person has the ability to literally consume the other person; therefore, directing their thinking, influencing their choices, and planning their future. These aggressive people absorb another person's life in stride. As long as the captive stays in stride, all is well. The abused must follow a narrow path without deviating from the master's plan. Should a deviation begin or a different situation begin happening, the perpetrator articulates this to other people subtly indicating a weakness in character of the abused. Or, by voicing a slight concern about that person to other people, manipulation continues with the unsuspecting listener. One explanation given a listener infers that the abused has become too dependent. After being groomed for dependency over time, to become dependent demonstrates weakness thereby lessening the attraction. Winning the person over, consuming them entirely looses its excitement when they have won. They use their articulation skills to keep themselves in good standing with other people and stand ready to defend themselves or humble them-selves if need be. If they are suspected of having an inappropriate relationship, the humility card works well to evoke sympathy. Even though they initiated the relationship, it's never entirely their fault.

Naivety plays a prominent part in becoming trapped into an all-consuming situation. Guilt rolls in cutting off communication with others. Passion fertilizes the emotions awakening a desire for more intimacy, thus more time together. The desire to please that person becomes paramount to everything else. After all, they build confidence through flattery and through boosting the ego.

How presumptuous of one person to think he or she can consume another! But, given the right circumstances, he or she can succeed at least for a time.

Thank God the chain was broken. Though I suffered a tremendously embarrassing and traumatic event that ultimately ended the fascination, I feel my life was spared yet again. So, many years ago I embarked on a new fascination. It's called life. If I continued my story, an array of experiences would follow. But, I would loose the purpose driving me in this writing - to sound the alarm. Unsuspecting young people can and will attach themselves to an unlikely predator. The threat of harm may not be imposed as in child abuse or in marital abuse, but the "fear" factor existed as in the other scenarios. At that time in my life, I wouldn't have exploded with, "Hey, what are you doing?" I'd been taught to respect my elders. Her secret passion remained safe with me because of her confident personality and church status. I dared not mention this unbelievable turn of events to anyone.

Who would ever suspect a middle aged woman, the mother of two children, a faithful church member, and a respected business woman in her community, as having the ability to manipulate another person through sex? Inconceivable thought? An inconceivable event unless one has experienced the spider's web of cunning and desire. Inconceivable unless one has been clasped and tightened in the snare of a predator's trap. Be not deceived by appearances, by well-articulated speech, or by church affiliation as an older person proffers compliments and promises of new experiences that offer change from the ordinary.

The years 1967 into the 1970's signify the times most influenced and affected by Hilda. Even though I moved on, the manipulative, all-consuming obsession directed toward me by an unlikely predator forever lives in my memory. I came in contact with an unlikely predator who changed the course of my life. Eventually, my course survived the storm, but the effects linger even today.

www.ingramcontent.com/pod-product-compliance
Lightning Source LLC
Chambersburg PA
CBHW062149020426

42334CB00020B/2550